Self-Care for the Self-Aware

A Guide for Highly Sensitive People, Empaths, Intuitives, and Healers.

Dave Markowitz

BALBOA.
PRESS
A DIVISION OF HAY HOUSE

Balboa Press books may be ordered through booksellers or by contacting:

Balboa Press
A Division of Hay House
1663 Liberty Drive
Bloomington, IN 47403
www.balboapress.com
1-(877) 407-4847

Printed in the United States of America.

ISBN: 978-1-4525-7856-9 (sc)
ISBN: 978-1-4525-7857-6 (e)

Balboa Press rev. date: 7/31/13

"*As I read through the pages of Dave Markowitz's,* Self-Care for the Self-Aware *my heart opened wide because it felt as if he'd written this treasured little book just for me! Learning how to use my empathic abilities as a gift is something I have struggled with all my life. But my struggle is over now; what Dave Markowitz offers is the gift of absolute scripture, for those of us who are empaths. It is brilliantly simple, incredibly inspiring and profoundly effective.*"

~Kathryn Peters-Brinkley, Bestselling Author, Publisher of Kinetics Magazine.

Acknowledgments

Thank you to those who have stood behind, next to, and in front of me. I know the value of a great support system and I've attracted one of the best.

Gratitude to my Portland co-workers Joan D'Arcy and Peggy Rollo, publisher Kathryn Peters-Brinkley, Dannion Brinkley, Barry Goldstein, Dr. Meg Blackburn-Losey, agent Devra Ann Jacobs, BMSE, Findhorn Press for publishing my first book, and all those at Balboa Press for making this book possible.

Gratitude to the families: Markowitz; Mazza; Levin; Richman; and Lee; and to my soul families in/from New York and Portland.

Gratitude to all my clients, who I continue to learn from every day.

Special *Thank You* to my sweetheart, Maria. Your unconditional love has made me feel things I didn't know I could feel.

Front cover's self-hug image courtesy of www.JanetCristenfeld.com.

Author photo by Theresa Pridemore of www.cogflower.com.

Edited by Holly Wells.

Preface

For those who have not read my first book, *Healing with Source: A Spiritual Guide to Mind-Body Medicine*, I'd like to share with you that I went into alternative methods of healing kicking and screaming. I was pretty convinced that what I'd been doing— what I'd been taught—was right, but something much bigger than the Dave part of me kept me searching for deeper meanings and understandings. If someone had told me what was written in that book years prior to its creation, I would have quickly dismissed both that information and the messenger. Surely, only quacks would claim that repressed fear, anger and grief could cause illness. But years of experience and an intuitive message called *Healing with Source* made it all pretty clear. It was and is true. Even more wonderful was the awareness that by getting in touch with and embracing the raw emotions that most of us were taught not to show—by moving energy actively or passively—healing can begin. And by understanding the emotional underlying causes, we could also be empowered in preventing pains and illness from manifesting or recurring.

As is always the case, we must be ready to expand our consciousness and belief systems; we are here to grow with the flow. I wondered what would be next and then it hit me in a most unusual circumstance: I became aware that I can absorb the negative energy of others enough to become ill myself. And so can you. If someone had told me just a few years ago what you are about to read in *Self-Care for the Self-Aware*, once again, I would have quickly dismissed both that information and the messenger. Personal experience is all I have to go on. I was not and still am unaware of other books that explain what I'm about to share with you. I'd heard references to empaths absorbing energy, and I'd heard some techniques to prevent that, but none of them worked for me. And I saw that ultimately, they didn't work for others either. I knew there had to be something else. And then it showed up in "High Definition," crystal-clear visions and intuitively guided information for just about all of my clients over a the last few years. Just ask and it is given, right? But not on our terms. And maybe not in our preferred way or at our desired time. But it does show up. All you have to do is listen. You do know how to listen, don't ya?

Blissings and gratitude,
Dave

Table of Contents

Introduction

em·pa·th / émp'æTH/ *N*: a person who can experience the thoughts, emotions, energy and direct experiences of others

Many people identify themselves as empaths, but few know how to use this skill effectively. When understood and used correctly, the burden of empathy can be a divine gift for the betterment of all humankind. After years of misunderstanding and denial, the author was forced to better comprehend his empathic abilities in the most unusual of circumstance. The catalyst was an atypical evening with friends in several bars. Not having drank anything other than water the entire evening, Dave Markowitz got drunk.

This opened up a whole new wave of clients in the following years. Over 90% of them had seen multiple practitioners yet still suffered from acute and chronic conditions. Their hopes of healing, their bank accounts, and their trust and faith in themselves, medical practitioners, and sometimes their higher power were constantly getting crushed. Medical doctors to shamans hoped for the best, but the best these clients could receive was an occasional and temporary relief of the symptoms. True healing could not be found. Clearly, something was missing.

What was missing is now found.

Dave's new bevy of clients had three distinct commonalities:

- they'd done a large amount of self-growth and healing work yet nothing had permanently shifted their pain or illness;

- they had an overblown sense of responsibility;

- and they were all empathic.

These clients often wondered why they were still unwell, having done all of the things recommend by the experts. Dave danced on the shoulders of the giants in the field, and was able to intuit that a combination of the above-stated commonalities were a recipe for much more than a temporary sharing of energy and emotion typically associated with empathy. There was an addictive quality to being an emotional and energetic sponge. The author believes that most of us are untrained empaths, and what untrained empaths take in—stays in. This led to pains and illness that could not be traced, understood, or healed by conventional or even well established alternative methods of healing. Simply put, the empath's symptoms were not their own.

For example, if a friend is going through a difficult time, I naturally want to help out. As an empath, I can absorb the energy of my friend and begin to feel what he's feeling. In a small amount, this can be a great thing; it can increase my compassion. But over time, an untrained empath can unknowingly develop symptoms of pain and illness that have an origin outside of the personal self; compassion is usurped by empathy due to a misunderstanding and misapplication of responsibility. The author knows this absorption process to be true because when energy is returned to its original source through a method described in this book, the empath heals even long-standing conditions.

We all know that metaphysically speaking, we are all one, but oneness does not have to include a lack of boundaries and an unhealthy empathic response. To do so is an invitation to become dangerously enmeshed with others. Empaths typically and often unconsciously avoid certain situations and people to prevent this unhealthy enmeshment. At best they have applied commonly accepted techniques that the author has found to only be useful in the short term; however, when using these walling techniques, there is no deep-seated learning or permanent transformation. *Self-Care for the Self-Aware* details vastly healthier responses for the empath. It offers linear, easily applied, long-term protective solutions so that the empath doesn't take on or keep unwanted energy.

Self-Care for the Self-Aware documents five powerful concepts and simple corresponding action steps. Dave intuited these to help himself and other empaths see our burdens transform into healings and realizations. Empaths learn that their skills—when worked with as described in the book—are a divine gift that can benefit all of humankind. Through detailed concepts and action steps, this book teaches the readers how to prevent themselves from becoming an emotional sponge, and introduces an incredible powerful exercise called *Return to Sender* that harmlessly "gives back" the misplaced energy, emotions, and more to their original owner with permanence. *Return to Sender* as described in the book provides immediate shifts and incredibly effective long-term results. The author states that in almost two decades of healing work, he has never seen a more powerful exercise that offers so much clarity to an often-desperate client. Overall, this work lets the empath know they're not alone, and that there is hope for what they've learned to believe was hopeless. This book can help you transform illness into health, eliminate pain and embrace freedom, and convert confusion into clarity and direction.

Stage One:

We Are Healers

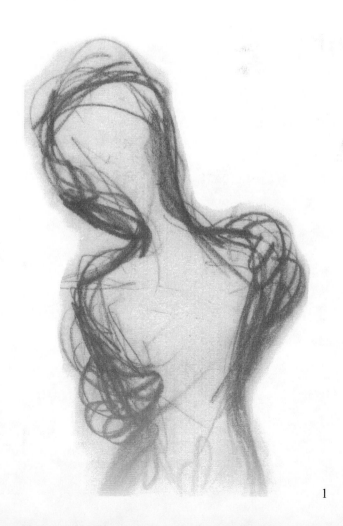

Chapter One:

Why We Find Each Other

"How many of you feel like the oddball in your family of origin?" That's what I ask attendees at almost every lecture I've ever given, and whether it's asked to a group of 20 or 2,000 attendees, about 90% raise their hand. And I think the other 10% are shy or can't raise their hand because they have shoulder problems.

If you're reading this, you already know you're different. You're deeply affected by what others seem to let go of so easily. The hurting of others hurts you emotionally and viscerally. The prevalence of judgments over unconditional love affects you. The waste of lives, resources, and time hurts you as you watch far too many people go about their lives on autopilot, in collective denial, or worse. Maybe you sometimes think (or know) you're from another planet.

We sensitivities see hypocrisy. We *feel* what's really true and what isn't. We hear voices driven by ego, feel hearts overpowered by minds, and see linear insular thought dominate over creativity. Perhaps when you were young, you used to think that everyone else was just like you were—kind, compassionate, and connected—but soon you learned otherwise. Now we know that not everyone else feels so deeply. Not everyone can feel beyond what the physical senses can perceive. Not everyone is aware of energy, auras, past lives, etc., but we—perhaps always or perhaps only over the last decade or year—know these things intimately. On the positive side, these differences make us wonderfully interesting. And on the negative side, these differences lead to alienation, isolation, and ill health that no one can help heal.

Emotional Danger

Being this sensitive, this intuitive, this aware, can make us feel less accepted and less understood. In difficult times, we're less likely to find heart-felt, helpful guidance from within the limited systems that we grew up in. We're less able and/or willing to fit into the "norm." Society as a whole does not recognize who we truly are.

And that's why we find each other.

We know who to talk to and when as we seek quality interactions. When we enter a room, we immediately know who to approach and who to avoid. This knowing is usually unconscious—a by-product of awakening, of becoming more and more intuitive. We want to connect with and even help everyone we see, but find that trying to do so is too difficult or too draining. It is overwhelming to be so close to those in deep pain, so we either try to put a wall between the perceived "us" and the perceived "them," or worse, we turn away. And many of us would rather live alone or with animals than be in the constant presence of humans who don't understand us.

Simply growing up in a world that is so emotionally foreign and unsafe has forced us to develop coping mechanisms to get us through each day—beyond those self-protections every human needs to develop to some degree. This is a world that doesn't allow us to express ourselves as the love we now know we are. Even in the first few days of life, well-meaning parents or guardians attempt to distract us from feeling the sadness associated with our initial separation from multidimensional vastness, perfection, and love, into a limited corporeal form. We learn to protect ourselves from others' emotional limitations and inauthenticity by "checking out" or playing small, or distancing ourselves from others emotionally—and if possible—physically as well. Eventually, others who have dealt with these sensitivities and those in some of the healing arts tell us that we need to protect ourselves from potential negative forces. The walls we're told to construct are imagined to be made of impervious brick to truly separate, or glass so we can see what's there and still be protected, or a mirror that can reflect back to the person(s) what they're sending our way. And these work to some degree, but they also can block us from receiving the good things as well. If you've been wondering: "Where is my soul mate? When will I experience abundance? What is my perfect job?" they're likely just on the other side of the block you've placed in front of you!

Called to Be Healers

We are jigsaw craftspersons; we have an **intrinsic calling** to bring together the perceived pieces of the whole; to heal the hurt. We know there is peace within all hearts and if we could only open our hearts more and open the hearts of others, we could live in a glorious growth-inducing, peaceful world. Like driving with our feet on both the gas and the brakes, we desire this heart opening and other types of forward movement but are too often held back by fear or illness. We crave intimacy but isolate more than connect. We desire more joy and connection but don't always pursue it. And there is a reason for all of this.

Whether we think of ourselves as sensitives, intuitives, healers, nurturers, caregivers, or emotional or spiritual guides or practitioners, we all have in common the quality of "reading" and taking on other peoples' emotional energy. Whether we are aware of it or not, we are all empaths. (I'll use the terms "empath" and "empathic" as shorthand throughout the rest of this book to describe this concept or us.)

6

Even if you are not a professional healer, you are still a healer. If you're reading this, you've likely developed a big, open, nurturing heart and presence that makes you a really great friend to others. You always have an ear or a bit of wisdom for them. You are the person that other people seek, not always to talk *with*, but perhaps more often to talk *to*. You enjoy being a helper of any type and therefore do so, sometimes to your own detriment.

I've found that when this common quality of empathy is understood and worked with effectively, it makes our journey much easier. Awareness of this deep-seated ability and the knowledge of how best to use it lets things flow more smoothly and increases our spiritual awareness, our sense of connection, and even our health and vivacity.

Healing Others, Harming Ourselves

To differing degrees, we empaths feel the pain of others. We have consciously and unconsciously created survival mechanisms that try to minimize or even halt that empathy— the taking **as our own** the energy, pain, or situation of someone else. But those same defenses also prevent us from fully participating in and enjoying life. Despite our defenses, we still take on others' energy, take on their pain, illness, and responsibility, and are too often sick, or drained, or scared, or lonely, and can't seem to shake it. It is no wonder that we fear fully embracing our gifts and experiencing the immense overwhelm that we expect is likely to result. We don't dare cry out the grief we're already carrying because we fear it'll open a floodgate and we'll drown in a sea of sadness. This, ironically, can cause what some call "depression" —the repression of our own and others' grief that we carry within us. Learning how to use empathic abilities as a gift and not a burden is crucial to our full expression and optimal health.

New Skills

If a child has a proclivity for playing piano, he typically needs to study theory, composition, and arranging to express his musicality for its maximum effect and so that other performers can understand his intention. He needs to learn about interpersonal dynamics to play well with others. If taught effectively, these skill sets augment his abilities and allow him to be a terrific performer, teacher, or even sound healer—learning from interconnections rather than living in narrow separation. Likewise, we as empaths need to learn a skill-set to make sure empathic abilities are used for the positive, and do not become a cross to bear. As a medical intuitive "reading" underlying causes of pain and illness, I've become an expert at identifying other empaths and sharing tools that strengthen us at a basic, transformative level. Empathic abilities when misunderstood, misused, or ignored can drag us down emotionally, sometimes to the point of near-paralysis. They fatigue us quickly and perhaps even chronically, and burden us with unnecessary responsibility and ill health that doesn't heal no matter what we try. It is my intention to share tools to guide your transformation into being more emotionally expansive and healthy so that you can enjoy your lives and share your various gifts without fear of being overwhelmed by taking on others' emotional or physical pains or illness.

You're about to see on a deeper level that if we take on and identify with another's negative energy, we're not helping ourselves (obviously), but we're not helping the other person either. The latter was my personal "a-ha moment." In fact, even if our empathy is good intentioned, other people really don't want us to carry their burdens for them. Would you want your child or friend to carry your burdens?

What this book teaches is how not to be a sponge that takes on everyone else's pain or illness, while maintaining a healthy sense of connectedness. It explains why some of us are emotional sponges, what we can do about it, and how and when to squeeze out all the "stuff" we've accumulated from others. And it goes one step further and explains how to be so porous that we never truly absorb the dis-ease of others, while still being able to help them at new, more empowering levels.

Chapter Two:

It Takes One(ness) to Know One(ness)

For years I'd heard people speak of energy transference. In massage therapy school they mentioned it, but I didn't listen very intently. In new thought bookstores and at spiritual events—seemingly everyone else knew about being drained by others. Many warned me about it, but I didn't think it could happen to me. Oh, ego, I love you so!

I maintained this view, even though one of my first house calls as a New York-state licensed massage therapist left me with a headache worse than any I'd ever had. My client didn't know it yet, but he had advanced cancer. He only learned of his condition about a week after I saw him, and he transitioned out of his corporeal form not too long afterward. I was "picking up" the depleted, dark energy associated with his condition.

Years later, I still didn't want to own my empathic sensitivity; it seemed too "New Age" to me. I concluded that if I could maintain my strength, others just wouldn't affect me. But I isolated myself more than not. I avoided crowds, certain people, and situations that everyone else seemed to love. In actuality, I was unconsciously trying to protect myself from feeling the overwhelming fear, anger, and grief of others.

Unfortunately, limiting my life didn't limit my pain.

I Got Drunk to Clear My Vision

After a few months in a new city where I barely knew anyone, I was invited to a friend of a friend's birthday party: seven bars in seven hours on a party bus. I hadn't had alcohol in about a decade and avoided the bar scene pretty much entirely, but thought it might be a good opportunity to connect with new people. (I forgot how coherent speech dwindles proportionally to the amount of alcohol imbibed!) At the end of this night, having not had anything stronger than water, I was drunk! My words were slurred, my gait was uneven, and an odd sense of uncomfortable confusion permeated my mind. Amazingly, in the midst all of that confusion and discomfort, I finally realized just how empathic I was.

And I knew, almost immediately, that this lesson in empathy happened for a reason much larger than raising my awareness of the empathic abilities within myself. I had a deep intuitive knowing that my inquiries about how to deal with this would be answered somehow, in some way soon, and that this knowledge would need to be shared on a larger scale.

A New Kind of Client

After that evening, I began to notice that about 90% of my new clients had done a lot of work on themselves to advance spiritually and to heal themselves of a wide variety of physical and emotional pains and illnesses. Many could quote the best-selling spiritual self-help books (including my own!) word for word, many had tried varied and numerous modalities, but few had success in healing themselves. My medical intuitive readings repeatedly showed me that these clients were energy sponges and were carrying the negative and damaging energy of others within them. Even when doing all the "right" things, whatever symptoms were released in their prior attempts to heal with other practitioners—no matter how that was accomplished—were recreated over hours or days because of the symptoms' empathic origins. Even consistent sessions with one or various practitioners were ultimately unsuccessful because typical modalities— Western or Eastern—rarely permanently uproot and release the underlying cause.

My readings showed three commonalities too obvious to ignore: these clients were empathic; they had an unrealistic sense of responsibility; and they were far along on their spiritual paths. I have found that when these three qualities are combined, it is a recipe for ill health that never heals. My intention with this book is to provide a recipe calling for healthier ingredients.

The Problem With Oneness

Worldwide, many forms of spirituality talk about the reality of oneness. The idea is a beautiful one. The awareness of oneness is a staple of understanding the connectedness we all seek (yet already are). However, in this life, we are *finite* and unique expressions of the *infinite* One, and defining the necessary boundaries for the roles we take on is not a simple task. Seldom, if ever, are we taught healthy, specific ways of living from oneness.

The thought of being connected to our lover or to friends and family is wonderful. The awareness that someone in North America has shared atoms with someone in India or at the South Pole is mind-expanding and humbling, and even appeases and sparks our left-side, linear-thinking brain. But as either an alternative or allopathic healthcare practitioner, or as anyone who is nurturing, intuitive, or simply empathic, the very same connectedness that can open and expand the heart can also become a major pathway to finding and picking up the energy that creates ill health.

We all probably have experienced and valued connectedness, but when oneness is not applied to daily life in an empowering way, a host of problems can arise. The rules of quantum physics, or the microcosm, are very different from the rules of standard physics, or the macrocosm. Likewise, oneness has more than one aspect. We are all connected metaphysically, but physically we are not, nor should we want to be. If I'm connected physically to my clients, I'm going to have a very long day. If I'm too close to anyone without being aware of boundaries, the resulting enmeshment is unhealthy for all. As much as I love so many of you, I do not wish to merge with any or all of you enough so that your problems become my problems. Not because I'm mean or unsympathetic, but because quite simply your problems are not mine and it is not in my own or your best interests for me as a practitioner or even as a good friend to take on your "stuff." Therefore it is imperative that we fully understand the concept as it is and as it isn't, and apply that knowledge to our daily lives.

Chapter Three:

But I've Done So Much Spiritual Work; Why Am I Still Unhealthy?

"But I've done so much spiritual work; why am I still unhealthy?" Does that sound familiar? It was and has been a credo of many if not most of my clients over the past few years. No matter what their symptoms were—and they were as varied as the people themselves—they either said or I intuited (or both) that they had indeed done a tremendous amount of spiritual work, but they were still unhealthy.

It made little sense to the linear mind. If one wishes to achieve X, then one typically would find out how to get there from any number of various resources. You might read to do steps A, B, and C, and after those are applied, you should achieve X. A more tangible example would be studying a new language; you know there are time-proven steps to take. Learn the letters, their sounds, the words, and then syntax, and stream them all together and you're now speaking Spanish.

Most of my clients during this time were doing steps A, B, and C. Some were doing A through Z! They were already doing the "right" things but received no more than temporary—at best—results. They were receiving energy healing (often from numerous practitioners over many years), and/or they'd visited many doctors and therapists of differing types. Many were repeating affirmations, and most were forgiving those who've done them wrong and (hopefully) forgiving themselves. Others were taking herbs and supplements, and many were practicing spiritual principles of love and compassion to the best of their ability and so on, but they were still unwell.

A New Insight

Most readings painted a similar picture. I intuited and shared with my clients that **little if any of their emotional or physical pains or illness were their own!** As empaths, they were picking up energy from other people and taking it on as their own. It became clear to me that if a client were to do even a tremendous amount of spiritual and healing work, but did not know how to handle the gift of empathy, no matter what we did together and no matter what they'd done with a myriad of other practitioners and modalities, the symptoms of their illness would be recreated shortly after they were cleared. To help both them and myself, I intuitively began to develop the tools I now call "Steps to Preventing and Healing Empathic Pain and Illness" detailed in Stages Two and Three.

Many of these people had spent far too many hours away from doing what they loved while on a search for their own healing. So many had spent vast sums of money on books, workshops, practices, and practitioners without achieving a permanent alleviation of symptoms. On the bright side, these practices often did result in temporary symptom relief. But to repeatedly use modalities that don't get to the core issue is not much better than visiting an ordinary pharmacy for temporary symptom relief. I'm not against relief, but was deeply grateful when I discovered a way to work at the level of cause-based healing.

The Many Ways to Mask Symptoms Instead of Healing Them

A modern pharmacy is filled with hundreds of products that are designed to stop us from feeling physical symptoms. The vast majority of these products are designed to mask the pain at any cost and to catalyze temporary relief for the user as soon as possible. This gives the illusion of being healed, but depending on what's being addressed, we're not really healed after taking a pill.

We're told that if we have diarrhea, to take this pill. Runny nose? Take this. Have a cough or a headache? Take this. They're all designed to stop something very natural from happening and can cause more problems in the long term than what has been masked in the short term.

For example, diarrhea is often the body's reaction to food toxicity or to emotional toxicity while eating. But it doesn't feel good, so we take a pill to stop it from happening. Obviously, this keeps the toxicity within. A runny nose is often repressed grief trying to make its way out, and we take a pill to prevent that, too. A cough is often grief and/or throat chakra issues coming to the surface for healing, and a headache is often the end result of a chain reaction of tightened neck muscles that reduce the flow of blood, oxygen, and qi (energy) to the brain caused by mental, physical, or emotional distress. But instead of allowing the body to heal itself by detoxifying naturally, or dealing with the grief, or communicating our truth, or dealing with what's stressing us, we take a pill. It's temporary symptom relief by design. Sadly, the metaphysical pharmacy isn't much different.

In the metaphysical pharmacy, we take natural supplements, homeopathic and herbal tinctures, get bodywork, receive one or more of the myriad of types of energy work, take a workshop, and read books to feel better. Most of these are designed to get us out of pain or discomfort as well. Most are not covered by insurance, and are therefore considered costly. But the true cost can include much more than your time and money.

In the long term, going to the metaphysical pharmacy and/or using the standard pharmacy's medications can affect our health in negative ways. While some alternative supplements and modalities are designed to boost the immune system, they too do not always address the underlying cause or causes of distress, not asking, for example, what is causing the immune system failure? So, by design, many of the metaphysical pharmacy's services or products as well as the standard pharmacy's products bury symptoms so they're no longer in our conscious awareness, though there is the benefit of fewer side effects with alternative medicine. Which brings up the question: What are "side effects" anyway?

If you take a pill to stop X and do achieve temporary symptom relief without the underlying energy being released, the same underlying causative energy will sometime thereafter make itself known. It may look very different from X that is now masked, so we'll call it Y. Then, we'll take a pill to relieve ourselves of the symptoms we're calling Y. The same underlying causative energy that caused Y will be masked by the second pill, creating other symptoms that will appear later on. It may look very different from Y that is now masked, so we'll call it Z. And so on.

Covering up symptoms is only one of the shortcomings of taking pills; less obvious side effects exist as well. The energies of the pharmacist, the drug store, the distribution network, and those who make, design, package, and market the pill are within all medications. We unconsciously ingest all of that energy just like we absorb negative energy of pesticides and of animals that have been injected with growth hormones, antibiotics, or eat GMOs. Included in that "food" is the toxic energy of victimization and inhumane treatment. We also take in the emotional pain of the factory farm workers that inflict the abuse. We absorb those stress-related toxic biochemicals as much as the emotional pain of the manufacturers and marketers of the pills.

Whatever we ingest, whether a necessary medication or food, I would suggest that you bless it before you eat it. Say grace, express gratitude, and smile! ☺ This can raise the vibration of yourself and whatever you are ingesting, and in some cases can minimize side effects. And no, that's not permission from me to eat processed, radiated, pesticide-laden foods, or to take pills for every little discomfort!

Some New Answers

The answers that came to me for healing the causal energies that I share below, when applied, have been extremely effective in helping intuitives, caregivers, practitioners, sensitives, nurturers, empaths, teachers, healers and more clear out the pain they hold and have continued to take on from others. For example, a woman who'd been dealing with what she called chronic fatigue for ten years claims to have had dramatic improvement in just four days. Another woman was completely pain-free in just one session after five continuous months with debilitating headaches. Most experience a sense of lightness, more energy, more emotional freedom, fewer symptoms, a reduction or elimination of pain, less sense of burden or responsibility, and more awareness of what's truly important to them. While there is no one-size-fits-all for anything, these guidelines are extremely important for anyone with empathic skills.

Stage Two:

Preventing Empathic Pain and Illness

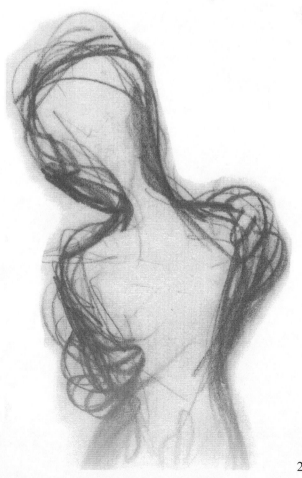

Chapter Four:

Release Responsibility

"You shifted my focus from thinking I had responsibility for any other living thing to thinking about what I might like to do with my life. Focusing on my own intent for my life with a sense of adventure and a goal of joy liberated me. I held onto that image of the hole in my heart chakra (See "Keyhole" exercise forthcoming), where everything that wasn't mine (at least 90% of everything!) could just pass right on through—no questions asked, no judgments made. I could feel the wind whistle through that hole unobstructed, on its way to meet the Sun. I never felt so much a part of the entire natural forces and so separate from the human-created ones. That's life! And all from one session. You told me I didn't need another one. I had gotten it. And I felt that way, too."

~Jane Peranteau, Project Manager, Albuquerque, NM

The Concept

I am not responsible for the soul path of another person.
Neither are you. You may know this consciously, but odds
are really high that as an empath who has not yet mastered
releasing other peoples' energies, you haven't fully embodied
this awareness.

The patterns of responsibility start early on. For some, it
begins in our first few days in the womb. We know now
that if a mother smokes, her baby smokes, too. But what
we don't often recognize is that if a mother is depressed,
the baby also shares that chemical imbalance. In our first
nine months of life, we grow, expand, and become aware of
what's happening with/within/for/to our mother, including
sensing her fear, anger, and grief.

After birth, we are still very connected to Source energy.
Even though we haven't yet mastered our visual acuity,
our inner awareness now expands to beyond the internal
environment of the womb. We believe that the people "over
there" are a part of us—mother, father, siblings, aunts and
uncles, doctors and nurses. At some level we "know" we can
and therefore begin to heal those closest to us in any way we
can. We don a "spiritual superhero cape" and get to work.

We learn that our joyful actions lighten the room and that our
sadness darkens it. So we utter nonsensical sounds, giggle,
smile—anything to heal, or raise the vibration of those around
us. The grooves of responsibility are formed very early on as

we see that anything we do affects those closest to us. At the same time, our small selves are learning how to experience our own emotions. Unfortunately, our cries are sometimes met with even more fear, anger, and grief from those around us. We are often given a pacifier when we cry, which both teaches us that it's not okay to express grief, and sets up patterns of oral satisfaction that later can become addictions used to temporarily quench fear and grief. Our anger, likewise, is thwarted in various—and ultimately unhealthy—ways.

We learn that things are very different when we are in the body from when we were in spirit form, and it saddens us. We also want to be our own person, so the ego begins to form in an attempt to separate us from the individual and collective pain of others. Because that process is not supported, we develop our own fear, anger, and grief. None of these expressions are supported either, causing the ego and sense of separateness to become more and more developed. But our sense of responsibility for making others happy and well persists. The spiritual superhero cape has become a second skin.

Self-Blame Extinguishes Self-Love

A few years later, if a caretaker or another relative living with you was unwell in any way, you sometimes took on responsibility for those conditions. For example, if your mother was depressed or your father was an alcoholic, the childlike mind now learning to deal with responsibility, thinks, "If I were a better child, Dad wouldn't drink and Mom would be happier, too." Many of us began doing what others wanted us to do in order to be loved and perceived as "good." This can manifest in "positive" or "negative" emulation to align with our caregiver(s) actions. For example, a child may become compassionate like his mother or stubborn like his father. Because the actions are in alignment with what the parent may say or do, the child is then called "good." Being good may get us love and attention, but getting love because of what we do or don't do is the very definition of conditional love, a very low vibration. This creates an unhealthy pattern that sets up all kinds of defeatist patterns for relationships later in life. As children, especially, we wished others around us to be happy and well. So we danced, acted extra "silly," and eventually told jokes, or used art, or good grades, or making dance or sports teams to get love from our caregivers or make them and others proud of us—to alleviate THEIR fear, anger, and grief!

While taking care of others before ourselves may go along with the *modus operandi* many of us were taught since childhood, the healthier spirituality sees this as an unhealthy martyrdom. I find it unfortunate that complete selflessness is regarded as saintliness, and the helpers are so busy giving that they do not take time to receive. Being poor or frail as an end result of this martyrdom is seen as a blessing, but I say that health and abundance are our birthrights. "It is better to give than receive" is an old paradigm that is by its nature, unsustainable, yet so many of us fall into the trap. Wonderful healers and compassionate folks go hungry while other people and larger organizations thrive, and it's because we fail to question the existent paradigm of selflessness. In fact, if we honor ourselves, we're considered selfish, and most of us were taught that selfish is the last thing to be or to be perceived as. And yet to do otherwise is unhealthy for the individuals whose intentions are loving and positive. I say to you, that honoring your own needs is the highest form of love. Not at the expense of others, but along with them. We can better serve others after we honor ourselves as children of God and start acting like we are worthy of that reality. To dishonor ourselves, to live from false humility, and to not recognize our worth, I believe, is the ultimate insult to the creator and will keep us in a perpetual state of discontent and wanting.

None of this is meant to sound crass, but rather a wake up call to living beyond the smaller vision we were taught and to begin seeing the bigger picture. It is better to love someone and their path unconditionally; it is better to be guide, a confidant, a wingless angel (though some of you have wings; I apologize if I've offended you) and whisper or scream words of encouragement and support rather than take on what's not yours. To take a part of another is thievery, but you both have been burglarized. Remember that another's grief is theirs, not yours. In fact, your benevolent intention has resulted in malevolent results. It's time to return to wholeness with this awareness.

The subconscious desire to heal one or both parents or caregivers becomes pervasive throughout life and expresses itself in a variety of ways. The overweight parents raise the son or daughter who wants to become a nutritionist or personal trainer. The narcissistic father raises the daughter who becomes a psychologist, social worker, or other form of counseling practitioner in order (subconsciously) to understand what makes him tick. The superficially inclined parent raises a child who wants to explore and go deeper, and who often becomes an academic or intuitive—a seeker of truth. The grief-stricken mother gives birth to the child who becomes an energy healer or a comedian.

As adult children, we often try to heal a parent, directly or indirectly, but it can't be done. Nor is it our job to do so. No matter how successful we may be in our healing modality or other vocation, subconsciously there is turmoil because no one can truly heal another. No matter how successful we may be in any career, there is turmoil because it's being done for the wrong reasons. This leads to fears of not doing/being enough. No matter how much good work we do in the world, the underlying impetus to become an effective healer or even successful businessperson can never be satisfied.

People do anything to fill an emotional void that is within them. Weapons of "mass distraction" are plentiful and readily available. We drink, smoke, overeat, get lost on the Internet, or heal others to cover our own pain—to fill that hole. But it doesn't work. Extreme examples of this behavior are addictions. While some addictions appear better or healthier than others (exercise is seen as better than drinking alcohol, but excessive exercise can be as damaging as alcohol), they're all rooted in the same need that can never be satisfied by actions that don't address our true need, which is for wholeness, connection, and self-acceptance—the exact things we believe we want from our caregivers but feel we can never get enough of.

The sense of responsibility that most babies learn, when combined with being an empath, makes us absorb the problems and take on the imbalances in others. We typically try to heal others ahead of maintaining a healthy practice of self-care. Some of us burn out after barely a decade in a field that, if chosen and performed with awareness and use of the steps suggested in this book, could last a lifetime. If we get paid to be a healer of any type, or receive any other form of strong positive reinforcement, it's even harder to let go of the learned sense of responsibility from infancy. Our ego identification is with being a helper and that, combined with the unrealistic sense of responsibility, creates a one-way exchange of negative energy that we take on and hold onto—sometimes forever.

When Helping Others Doesn't Really Help Them

No one really wants us to take on his or her problems, especially a parent. On a higher-self level, it is actually contrary to a parent's karma to allow a child to take on the parent's woes. For example, if you carry your father's (or friend's, partner's, or client's) anger, we're not helping ourselves, obviously—but we are also not helping him. His anger and all the physical end results that may have manifested in you (examples of repressed anger may include tight muscles, elevated blood pressure, tumors, heart disease, etc.) are his for a reason. We can identify that reason for him if he asks for such, but if he does or doesn't, we have to remember that it is his, not ours. If we take that anger from him, he no longer has that "warning light" that indicates that something within him needs to be addressed. Dad's underlying causative energy stays within him unnoticed, until it comes out again, likely as something slightly worse because of the accumulation and the lack of addressing it. Like sharing a drink with an alcoholic, we're enabling him. We are actually harming him in the long run—as much as ourselves—by taking on his issues.

Empathy vs. Compassion

The same actions done with differing intentions will produce dramatically different end results. For example, giving someone money out of pity (judgment, empathy) has a lower vibration than giving to him or her out of unconditional love (acceptance, compassion). The former can result in dependency for the recipient and an ego trip for the giver. The latter can result in self-reliance for the recipient and an ever-opening heart for the giver. Likewise, it's great to be a healer, it's great to have compassion, but when compassion is overshadowed by empathy it becomes far less healthy or even helpful. Being a healer—with or without a title or degree—from a place of empathy is destructive to both parties. Empathy is an emotion of responsibility and enmeshment—a very low vibration, and comes from a misapplication of the concepts of oneness and responsibility. However, being a healer from a place of compassion and the more complete understanding of oneness is a higher vibration. Compassion is a sharing of unconditional love. It is channeling Universal energy for the good of all through a physical form called a healer. A master that we can all relate to is His Holiness the Dalai Lama. If he were to feel responsible for all those who think he is responsible for them, he would be dead by now. But instead of empathy, he's mastered compassion, and anyone in his presence can feel that. Anyone in his presence can feel his lack of judgment and his correct application of the concepts of oneness and responsibility.

Responsibility or Love?

How do you know if you are coming from responsibility or from love? If you think you're indebted to help someone, feel uninspired or are drained during or after being of help, it's likely coming from responsibility. This also includes acting from guilt, shame, or fear; they all lead to resentment, and a constriction of your energy and thus a reduction of your immune system's capabilities. If you feel more joyous, openhearted, and energized during the action, it's coming from love. Actions when channeled through the body from infinite Universal love cannot tire you. Actions coming from a sense of limitation, responsibility, guilt, shame or fear certainly will block energy flow leading to stagnation, discomfort, and eventually pain and/or illness.

None of this means to ignore or to stay clear of those in emotional or physical pain. It only means we need to understand that their pain isn't our pain, and that it is NOT our job to fix it for them. In fact, us carrying their burden prevents them from truly healing. It is best to be a supporter, a guide, an assistant to a process, but not a sponge or an enabler. There is a very big difference.

Not taking on responsibility, of course, is situational. This is not an excuse to let our children harm themselves or others out of ignorance. We are responsible to some degree for our children, including clothing and feeding them, giving them love, and making sure they're safe. But they have much to learn on their own. How many of us have told a teenager not to do a certain thing only to watch him do that very thing we've been warning him about, and had it end horribly? It is difficult to watch and experience, of course, and yet that teenager has learned a powerful lesson through first-hand experience, which is a better teaching than even the most loving parents can provide through words alone.

Honoring Others' Paths

We're talking about a much bigger perspective, about living from a soul-level awareness that truly understands spiritual paths and honors all people wherever they are. It may be part of your path to help others, but again, not from a place of responsibility; that is actually power tripping and filling our egos with a belief that we are doing the healing. We are not. While people feel that I am a high quality healer, I rather believe myself to be a high quality channel—one who can open himself up and let Universal energy pass through me via my intention like liquid through a funnel to a desired end. The less attached and the more loving my intention, the better the results.

The compassionate person loves others as they are, where they are, and who they are. We can better achieve this state by trusting the bigger picture. We have to know deep within our cells that all people are exactly where they need to be. We should not judge another's path; according to many mystic traditions, their soul has chosen the perfect vehicle for them to fulfill their mission. No matter what's happening on the outside, on the inside the soul is having the time of its life! It's best to offer guidance or love or a safe listening space or a book recommendation or a few dollars or a hug because it's what we're called to do from a higher place, not out of low vibration actions. We then should drop all attachments to outcomes, even if you are being paid to be in service.

The Action Step

We need to integrate a mental awareness of **compassion over responsibility** deep into the cells so that it becomes a habit and not just a thought. New ideas become habits through conscious repetition of thoughts, words, and actions. Regularly repeat to yourself that compassion means to accept everyone exactly where they are, with no need for others to be, say, or do anything in particular.

Do you remember the first time you drove a car? There were a lot of steps to be aware of, to remember, and to implement and at first it seemed overwhelming. But after a few months, those steps became habit. And now, years later, you can arrive somewhere not remembering the drive you took to get there. Discerning between compassion and empathy—and learning who and what we're responsible for—isn't much different. The process can take moments, days or months of conscious awareness and repetition—there is no right or wrong or even typical amount of time—it will take what it needs to. The important thing to remember is that NO ONE IS RESPONSIBLE FOR ANOTHER PERSON'S SOUL.

There are other practices that can help spur the integration of the concept that no one is responsible for another. Experiential therapies that get to the emotions in the body can help. Also, you can write about it, meditate upon it, sing it, dance it; the awareness will integrate with conscious intention, patience, and action. In every way possible, affirm that, "I am only responsible for myself."

The specific action step is living mindfully—knowing what type of help to give or not give and knowing why or why not. A *compassionate "no"* may be in order. "I'm sorry, I don't feel comfortable with that" or even a "Not right now, maybe later" can work wonders, but typically we can best be heard when we speak that from a place of un-triggered emotions. By living mindfully, we can recognize an unresolved emotional trigger, let ourselves feel it to heal it (more on that later), and then have easy access to the higher truth. Example: "What you just said really triggered me, so I'm going to leave the room for a moment, and I'll come back to discuss it when I'm clear." This may sound difficult, but with practice it becomes easier. From that cleared place, it is very easy to know exactly what to say, be, and do in any situation. When open and clear, the perfect words and actions always follow because access to the heart is easier; the ego-based pain has been dissolved.

Resistance is Futile

Sometimes, subconsciously, we are unwilling to stop carrying the burdens of a loved one, even if he or she is deceased. The sense of responsibility is only deepened by the subconscious belief that another person (or soul if they're deceased) **needs** us to help them. We may feel that Mom or Dad is too weak and that if we return their fear, anger, or grief to them, they'll crash, and the guilt will be gut-wrenching. Not true; they need what is theirs. In fact; quite often, their pain becomes a catalyst to their growth.

Another form of resistance is when we're attached to being the sponge. If there is identification of being a healer, resistance is typical, but not irreversible. It will require a dismantling of your attachments to being in service for a loved one, small group, or community IN THE WAY THAT YOU HAVE BEEN ACCUSTOMED. Even if you don't consciously know who you are feeling responsible for, that information will ultimately make itself known to you if it is necessary for your healing and growth. Focus on sole/soul responsibility whenever possible. Write about it, talk about it, sing about it and dance it into your cells repeatedly; hourly or daily if necessary, and certainly before engaging with others. There is no one right way for everyone. Meditate upon the integration of this wisdom and eventually it will become a habit.

Both of these are a difficult belief to access; many of us hold these forms of resistance on deep, inner levels not easily reached by the typically functioning conscious mind, so we must be diligent in discovering what's true *at our core*. The deeper degree that you achieve this knowing, the easier it will be to heal what ails you and prevent reoccurrence.

Your success with the concepts and tools in the rest of this book will depend on your ability to know and integrate this message:

1. Metaphysically speaking, your primary responsibility is to yourself.

Chapter Five:

The Keyhole

"Thank you for today! I started using the process and have had good results already. I did step two (the Keyhole) as it was coming at me, let it pass through, felt the twinge of pain, and it was gone! I'm gonna keep practicing this and will cut myself some slack in moments that I stumble."

~Barb T. mother, student, Portland, OR.

Chapter four in this Stage described an awareness that must be integrated, to release our exaggerated sense of responsibility for others. Chapter five is more active, employing a consciously applied method to end our taking on and keeping others' fear, anger, or grief. This is required because essentially we empaths are "emotional sponges" who intuitively absorb everything around us, and we need to find a safe way to deal with this. Using this tool is a way to let others' energy flow through us and out, so that we don't take it on as "ours."

The Concept

We are nurturers, givers, and helpers. It's in our nature. It's far more satisfying, effective, and healthy to work with this divine nature than against it. Going with the flow is more empowering than going against it. Telling you to put up walls to protect yourselves—blocking the flow as is often recommended—also minimizes other, more positive people and circumstance intended for you. Because we can't selectively invite or block specific frequencies, it's best to **open to all the Universe offers us, keep what we like, and discharge what is not meant for us**.

Many of us have learned to block incoming unwanted energy by putting up a wall. As with many healing modalities (and general ways of being), this seems to be effective, so we don't question it. But it only works in the short term. This wall is the energetic equivalent of holding out our hands and arms to keep negative forces at bay. On a physical level, how long can we hold our arms up and outward in an attempt to block or push away a person? Not very long before exhaustion sets in, right? Metaphorically, this energetic pushing away tires us as well, and blocks the good gifts of Source from reaching us.

The Action Step: The Keyhole

Before entering a room or situation where you're likely to be drained, feel, visualize, or imagine your heart chakra opening. Then, like a keyhole in a door that lets a person see through and to the other side, feel, visualize, or imagine the front and back of your heart chakra open enough that if someone were looking at you from the front, they could see what's behind you through this opening. It can be open to the width of a grapefruit for more potentially difficult situations or people. It can be smaller, too. Make it the size of a raisin for what you may perceive as less emotionally painful situations. Then invite whatever negativity is coming toward you to go right through you and out the back. Do not let it hit the sides of the "tunnel," rather sense it entering the center space and flowing on through! You might feel the flow of energy as wind or you can imagine light, color, sound, or whatever works best for you, to allow unwanted energy to travel in and out in the same millisecond. I use a mantra, "I'm me, and you're you; whatever you send, I let go through." Feel free to use that one (royalty checks made out to my name, please!) or make up your own. It is really that simple yet remarkably effective. The heart chakra is already an active spiral, so envision a tornado on its side, pulling negative energy in and right out the back. We're not changing your divine blueprint of being an empath, just finding ways to use it so that you're no longer burdened with its potential ill effects.

I recommend the heart chakra because that is the seat of compassion for most. If your intuition tells you to use another chakra, feel free to use that instead.

The Keyhole is just one tool of many that my clients and I have found to be remarkably effective because you are working with the flow of energy as opposed to trying to block it. However, I do recall one instance where this was not effective. I was in a very small room with about 30 people and I had tried allowing whatever negative energy was coming my way to go through, but I still felt weakened. In that case, in my mind's eye I put up a wall and felt better pretty quickly, but I also remembered to take it down as I exited the building. So use your judgment, there is no one-size-fits-all in anything!

The Blessings of Being Empathic

Many of us who have not known these steps may have found our empathic abilities a burden. And many of my clients—burdened, drained, and ill—have asked me what the main advantage to being empathic is. My response is that with the ability to feel the emotions of others, when used correctly, empathy can increase your level of compassion toward others. Compassion is one of the primary precursors of enjoying an open heart and establishing truer connections with others. Compassion is a requirement for heart-centered relationships, authentic communication, and full emotional expression. Picture a world where everyone was more compassionate. Might there be less hunger, poverty, or war? You could be the forerunner of this vision, and empathy is your broomstick or magic wand; the choice is yours!

Discernment

It can be difficult to know what's yours and what is another's. This, like many other action steps of growth, requires practice and patience. When present, discernment is much easier.

Try to bring yourself fully into the moment. Sometimes doing something physical—like rubbing your hands together—increases the amount of sensations in *this now*, and can bring you into the moment. Then try to feel what's going on within you. With presence, you can actually ask it, "Are you mine or another's?" With practice, the answer becomes easier to see, feel, or hear. It's okay to feel momentarily the pain of another. This helps you walk in another's shoes even for a few seconds and increases the connection between you and the other, increasing compassion through shared experience or sensation. Then, let it go. Remember, it's not your job to be a sponge any longer.

Practice and Patience

Of course maximizing your efficiency with the concepts in chapters four and five takes practice and patience, but start a little bit each day and celebrate your successes! Some people get this in the moment; others may take years. While we of course want results quicker than slower, we can't rush change; to do so often creates more resistance. Work at this in your own perfect, divinely inspired time frame!

Releasing responsibility and using the Keyhole can change your pattern of taking on and embodying the fear, anger, and grief of others. It is, in my humble opinion, the most effective method of dealing with your own empathic abilities so they are blessing and not a curse. These two steps are the keys to preventing taking on empathic pain and can and should be done by each of us before engaging with others. If your sense of responsibility includes wanting to heal the world, I'd suggest working these steps at least once a day, hourly if need be. The mind will want to know how often and for how long. Give it a hug and invite patience instead. Just begin and let guidance take over. The deeper degree that you achieve this knowing, the easier it will be to heal what ails you and prevent reoccurrence.

Your success with the concepts and tools in the rest of this book will depend on your ability to know and integrate these:

1. Metaphysically speaking, your primary responsibility is to yourself, and

2. When engaging others, utilize the Keyhole!

The deeper degree that these steps are in place, the better the possibility that you can finally heal empathic pain and illness using the concepts in Stage Three.

Stage Three:

Healing Empathic Pain and Illness

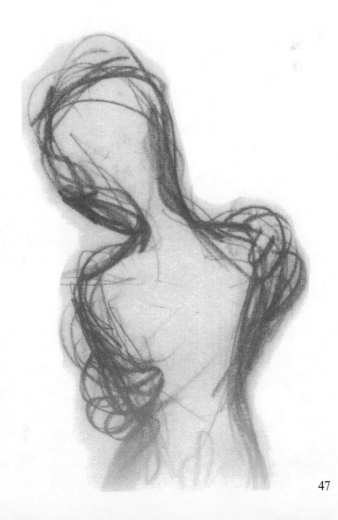

Chapter Six:

The Body Scan

The Concept

Now that we know we're not responsible for others, and we know how to stop taking on and keeping the fear, anger, and grief of others, it's time to release the months or decades of accumulated negative, stagnant energy that is very likely the underlying cause of our pain and illness; the "stuff" we've tried in so many ways to clear, but with only temporary success. We have to give back what's not ours.

As emotional sponges, many of us have made it an unconscious habit to take on the energy of other people. Clearly this affects us in negative ways. It drains us, manifests in pain and illness, and weakens our immune system to the point where we can barely fight off even a minor problem. One of the most interesting things—my personal "ah-ha moment" in all of this—is that while we may enjoy to some degree or even get commended or paid for being an empath, it's actually the last thing another person's soul wishes to happen.

Each soul has a mission, and by us taking on the energy of another person, that soul no longer has what it needs; it's actually incomplete! For example, if you carry your mother's sadness (or any physical results that may arise from repressing the sadness; examples may include digestive disorders, skin problems, lung issues, what's called depression, fatigue, etc.), she no longer has the impetus to go within and see what it's about. Her grief is a message, a challenge, and an opportunity for her to look at an aspect of her life that has not yet been examined. By you taking that from her, she will likely feel fine and may continue her unhealthy behavior. To use a motor vehicle analogy, she no longer has the dashboard warning light to tell her that something is in need of attention. She will likely feel better in your presence, but you will likely feel worse. Even if you decide to consciously be a sponge, the end results are the same; you feel burdened and she's still incomplete.

Resistance

When doing this process, you may become aware of your own lack of desire to return the energy.

Why? Because it's been part of you for a very long time, and you may not know what's on the other side of the return. As illogical is that sounds, many would rather be comfortable in their discomfort than take a chance on something new. It is said that the slaves that Moses freed asked to be returned to Egypt and live as slaves again rather than live in their new freedom because that included facing the unknowns of the desert. At least they'd know they'd regularly get a bite to eat as a slave, even if it was just a morsel. Sometimes, you just have to take the leap and deal with the ramifications later.

Why else? Because we fear that if we give back the baggage, then the other person will crash. Logical, but unlikely. **What's a huge burden for you is typically a mere drop in the proverbial ocean for them** because it's a return to the natural order of things. I've never had any client report that the person to whom they have returned their fear, anger, or grief has had a dramatic worsening of symptoms after the Return to Sender process you're about to begin.

Time Is on Your Side

Another very important thing to remember is that each person's process will be different. You may master this in a few minutes, or it may take a few years. Let it be like Yoga—ideally—where you accept wherever you are. By accepting where you are, you create room for growth and integration. By creating and then fighting the resistance, you give it more energy, and what you focus on expands, making this entire process much more difficult than it needs to be. I've had some people get this and have dramatic results in one session, others need a few months, and it's all fine. You can't rush this, just like you can't rush the fermentation time for your Kombucha; time really is on your side.

While some will do this as described below and have great results, others may need a more flexible and supportive guide to lead them through what could be a very challenging exercise. The template below will work well for most, but others may need a much more individualized approach. If the latter is the case, please contact me to set up an appointment. Like working with a personal trainer or life coach, I can help you work through the resistance and get better results faster than working on your own.

On the other side of these steps is a new level of freedom for you. And isn't that what we all want? Beyond the mind's ideas of what to own, what to look like, how to live, how to love, and how to do and be, what we really seek at the deepest level is liberation and freedom from the perceived constraints. We do this via a reconnection to our Source and by returning to the sender what's theirs and not yours. A new way of being will make itself known that is closer to that liberation. It may be uncomfortable at first, but true growth usually is.

If you've made it this far, odds are pretty high that you're carrying the negative energy of others. By doing the first step in the return process, called the Body Scan, you can ascertain if what you're dealing with is yours, or that of another, or a combination thereof, and the results of that inquiry will lead you to exactly the right thing to do.

Good or Great

The end results of the Body Scan and Return to Sender can be good or great. Good would be to have total clarity on exactly what has been ailing you and why you've not yet been able to heal. Great would be a reversal of the energy to its original source, leading to a reduction or elimination of the symptoms of empathic pain or illness at the causal root. All the steps in this book will happen when you are ready to allow them to. They cannot be forced. Each step herein can take seconds or several minutes. It is helpful to remember that your body is always trying to heal itself, and Source is always trying to give to you exactly what is needed for that to happen. All possibilities are always available in each moment, all you have to do is open up to them and allow their manifestation.

Action Steps

Have a pen and paper ready!

From a quiet, centered place, focus your attention inward. Start at the head and slowly move downward to the feet. Along that journey, typically one area will stand out above all the others. It may or may not even be where you expected it to be. Just go with what shows up. If two or more areas make themselves known, try to ascertain which is talking the loudest. Even if you guess incorrectly, good things can still come of it.

Remember that you can't actually cause anything to hurt by doing this; you can and are raising awareness of what's already happening within you. Once you are in tune with what's in need of attention in this moment, stay focused on that area.

Whose Grief is it Anyway?

Lets use an example of becoming aware of discomfort in the heart chakra. Stay with it and try to go one step deeper. Remember that all pain and illness is multi-layered, so you're just allowing a deeper awareness to be awoken. Under that discomfort will be an emotion. Allow that to come to you. Stay with that emotion and try to embrace it, it is not your enemy; it is a wound in need of healing.

Once that is identified, write it down. Example:

Under the discomfort in my heart chakra, I feel a sense of sadness.

Stay with the feeling, and when you're ready, try to feel even deeper into it. This may bring more discomfort but it is often necessary and always temporary. Once you are connecting with it on a deeper level, try to let an awareness of who it belongs to arise in your consciousness. You can ask it directly, "Are you mine, or that of someone else, or a combination?" Give it the time and space to answer as needed.

When you have that answer, write that down. Example:

Some of this grief is mine, but most of it is someone else's.

This is good. We now have awareness where before you had blanks. The next step is to determine whose energy you are carrying. Ask it for its original source. You may hear or feel or intuitively know the answer. Write that down. Example:

Most of this grief belongs to my mother.

If you get emotional, that's a good thing, just roll with it! Once you have this vision or feeling, sink deeper into that. Know that the reason you've been unable to heal is because you were looking for health in all the wrong places. And it's okay. You were never taught to look within. It's typical and not something to be ashamed of. At least now, courtesy of the Body Scan, you now have a new bevy of information and awareness to work with! It's time for the next step.

Chapter Seven:

Return to Sender

"Your Return to Sender exercise created a healthy closeness, instead of a 'healthy' distance! I was able to look in my mom's eyes and be more present with her in a way that she recognized and reciprocated. So I became MORE intimate with my mom and yet felt simultaneously LESS responsible. Can we say miracle? Let's say miracle."

~Laurell Eden, spiritual songwriter and teacher, New York

We are now conscious of the fact that many of us have been carrying others' emotional junk. So, logically, we have to return it to its original state, and I don't mean New Jersey. In the above example of carrying your mother's grief and/or the physical manifestations of such, her emotional baggage is hers, and at the highest level, she wants it back. Really.

You may not know right away who or what to work with, and that also is okay. Sometimes just by beginning the exercise, things become clearer. Whether it's the energy of your boyfriend, mother, father, sibling, cousin, friend, ex-partner, a small group or even a huge collective of people, know, on a very deep level, that what's theirs is theirs, and it's theirs for a reason. They need it. Whether this baggage is that of a person who is still alive or of someone who is out of their corporeal form, it's still theirs to deal with, not yours. The deeper degree that you achieve this knowing, the easier it will be to heal empathic pains and illness and prevent reoccurrence.

While the Return to Sender (RtS) ultimately can and should be done for everyone you feel you may be carrying a piece of (don't roll your eyes at me; I never promised this was going to be easy!), fill in the blanks with whoever comes up for you during the steps below. Trust the process. Call upon whatever higher power(s) you believe in to assist you. While I can assume that most of you believe in a higher power, there may be a few who do not, and that too is fine. I won't smack you over the head with my first book, or worse, a bible (it's much heavier) until you believe in a higher power; it's just helpful to know you are not alone and are being supported in your process. Source has no boundaries; when asked, it will help you in a way that resonates best for you. Feel that support that is always there, but is often buried beneath the conscious mind's thoughts and fears.

Action Steps

The action steps of returning unwanted energy to the original source is somewhat similar to an episode of Star Trek where the crew travels back in time to return the flow of events into the natural timeline. But you don't have to compute like a Vulcan to know what to do. All you have to do is follow this template. Once you Return to Sender that which is not yours, a whole new sense of freedom and health will arrive. Are you ready?

In your mind's eye, call upon the Highest Self of whoever showed up during the Body Scan. Allow their Highest Self essence to come to you; do not force it. Open your heart and connect with that vision, feeling, or impression non-verbally. Especially if this is someone you haven't seen in a while, take the time to take in his or her energy. Bathe in it, dance with it, and let it affect you emotionally. Be okay with whatever emotion arises, be it fear, anger, or grief, and embrace those, too.

Write the below to this person and feel free to make it your own by using words and phrases that are more in line with you, that person, or your relationship with them. Anything to the following effect will work:

Dear _____,

Thank you for coming to me in this way at this time. I am now fully aware that I have been carrying your _____ (pain, illness, fear, anger, grief, stress, etc.) in my _____ (back, shoulder, lungs, life, etc.).

I am now aware that I have unconsciously taken this on in an attempt to heal, support, or connect with you, or to get love from you. This was something I decided when I was younger that worked to some degree—but now no longer does. In fact, it has become an insoluble challenge.

Stay connected to the vision and watch for reactions. They may have something to say in response. Let them have their say, just like you wished they had given you the chance to speak in the past. Once the connection has been made in this way, typically they will appear softer and more open to you. Now you must begin the deeper work and ask them for permission to return to them what is theirs. Write the following, and again feel free to make it your own.

I have taken this issue on unconsciously and no longer need to. I am FULLY aware that this is yours to bear, not mine. In fact, I am aware that you are incomplete without it. My returning this to you, no matter how much that scares or excites either or both of us, must be done. Do I have your permission to return this to you at this time? And if yes, how much may I return?

He, she, or it will likely acknowledge what you are saying and grant you permission to Return to Sender that which is theirs. If you do not receive permission right away, remind them and you that this unnecessarily burdens you and you wish to return to them what is theirs. Ask if you can return a smaller percentage if necessary and be okay with any answer, if it's 50% or even 2%. If you get a percentage, that only means you have to repeat RtS the next day. Do this until you are really done, not when the mind says you are done. You will know when you are done when you feel it in your body, this can happen immediately, or not. Be patient; remember, time is on your side!

If you do not get permission to RtS, it is likely something on your end that is blocking the return, not theirs. Remember you are talking with another person's highest self, not their personality, ego, or their pain body, but the part of them that can love beyond the fears.

It is not atypical to have resistance; remember, some of you have been carrying other people's energy for decades, and it's oddly comforting to do so. But now is the time to stop the pattern. If not now, when? Reiterate to yourself that this is theirs, not yours, and that you are burdened by it and they are incomplete without it. Trust the process as best as you can and try again.

Once you get permission, begin the return. This may look like a gift basket full of fears or a warm open hug. I like to picture a file transfer similar to that which you'd see on a computer screen, or a tube of light; both can go on longer than a gift transfer until finished, but there is no right or wrong. As you do this, stay aware of their response and yours as well. Often you will feel lighter right away; it can even be an uncomfortable sense of lightness as this vibration could be something you have little to no recollection of being. Yet it may feel oddly familiar, closer to your original blueprint of divine perfection, freedom, and love!

If you did not receive permission, it is your issue, not theirs. No one's Higher Self would say no. You're more likely tuning into their personality or how you remember them. Try to go deeper past the personality and reach their Higher Self.

If this is ineffective, one possibility is that you have fears of the RtS hurting them. Re-read the above text, daily if need be, and really sit with that fear. The other possibility is that you've been identified with this pain for so long; you've worn your spiritual superhero cape for as long as you can remember! You're likely lost in, "Who will I be without this!?!?" even if it's unconscious. Well, remember that anything left in the dark cannot be healed. What's unconscious has to be made conscious to move forward. In this case, write that question down:

Who will I be without this?

Sit with the question and let an answer come to you. If you're viscerally oriented, you'll likely feel it in your body. If you're visual, you may see a vision. If you're emotionally open, you'll feel the answer. Write the answer below. Example:

I will better know who I truly am. I will feel free, happy, and whole.

Sink into the emotion of what you've written. While words can and do manifest a reality, feelings can do so quicker and on much deeper levels. Now, go back and do the Return to Sender exercise again. It is highly likely that you'll have a dramatically more effective experience. You will most likely feel a tremendous shift! Even if it's minor, congratulate yourself; you now know you're onto something huge and with repetition can create even deeper transformations daily.

If nothing has shifted, it only means you've yet to let go of the identification of yourself as an emotional sponge, and/ or release responsibility for others' burdens. In the good or great paradigm, this to me is still good. In time, when working with the causative energies, something has to give. It's really hard for some people to do this on his or her own. I even need someone co-creating safe space with me, and I've been teaching this for years! I know you want results, and you want them sooner rather than later, but some things can't be rushed. So be okay with your process and remember that it truly is a process, not an event.

Another possibility is that there is the equivalent of a detoxification, in that some symptoms may worsen. This is usually short-lived, and an invitation to relax and let your body catch up to the work. If it's exponentially worse, know that this process typically cannot cause illness, but can raise awareness of what's already there. Good judgment is needed here and if you're still unsure, perhaps a visit to an MD is in order. Use whatever modalities are available; there is no harm in going to a qualified practitioner, except perhaps to our egos that may be determined and attached to doing things its preferred way. All things, people, and events have a purpose; there are no mistakes. Use what feels right to use, while knowing both the potential advantages as well as the potential limitations of each.

Either way, congratulations, well done! Typically, you've just returned what does not belong to you to its original owner or you've identified why you were unable to continue the process at this time. Both options are better than where you were before reading this book.

This work isn't for the timid. Give yourself a pat on the back irrelevant to your expectation of success. Stop reading and do as you're instructed! Really, give yourself a pat on the back; it'll feel good. But don't get cocky, there's more to do. There's always more to do!

Chapter Eight:

Recalibration

If you were successful in your Return to Sender, part of you has just been transformed at a very deep level. And part of you has not. To align yourself fully, you will need to do a process of whole-self recalibration. While this is typically done with a practitioner, you can also do this on your own.

After Returning to Sender that which is not yours, you may feel light or relieved or even confused; there needs to be some time to integrate the new way of being. Similar to shavasana at the end of yoga practice, time is needed to acclimate, to celebrate internally, and to reconnect to your divine blueprint.

Give yourself this time, at least 15 minutes after the RtS, to sit in silence and let yourself feel whatever needs to be felt with a conscious intention of recalibrating to the new frequency. You may feel anything from sad to elated, and it's all fine. It's just a feeling and as much as we've been taught to bury our feelings, it's time to re-teach ourselves how important feelings are. Just have and embrace what's there.

On a more linear level of understanding what's happened, let's say you've been vibrating on a random frequency called 70. Part of you, perhaps your heart chakra, is now at 80, and we want to bring all of you to that higher level to match the lightness in your heart chakra. Doing so may feel uncomfortable, but that's okay and can be expected. Recalibrate after each and every Return to Sender for maximum effectiveness.

After recalibrating and listening to a felt-sense—or a deeper knowing—that this step is complete, you can celebrate on a larger scale. Go ahead, jump up and down a bit or roll down a hill on your side. Maybe even pat your back with both hands!

Recalibration can also further integrate the experience and the awareness gained in the first 4 steps (Responsibility awareness, the Keyhole, the Body Scan, and Return to Sender). Recalibration is useful in working with resistance as well; it can chip away at the stones of resistance slowly but surely.

If you're not feeling great or at least experiencing a lessening of symptoms after all of the above, that can be an indication that there's something still there that needs to be addressed. The next day tune in again to the area that is calling for attention and go through another Return to Sender experience. Some people release all of what's not theirs in one day, others take several months; just be okay with your experience. At some point, you'll know that what's *not* yours is gone, and then you can better address what *is* yours.

Stage Four:

Healing Our Own Pain and Illness

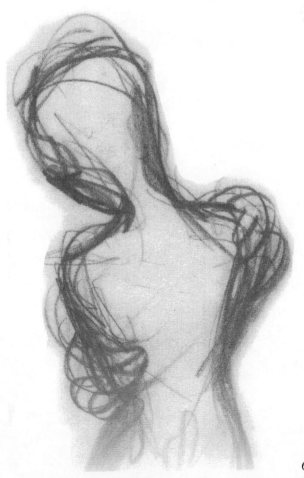

Chapter Nine:

Releasing What's Ours

Most of us know that repressed fear, anger, and grief stagnate our energy and produce symptoms of pain, discomfort, mental confusion, lethargy, illness, and so much more. So it is logical that releasing repressed grief, for example, will dissipate that energy and thus the symptoms.

We must address and challenge our old learned patterns of social behavior that say it's not polite, sexy, healthy, ladylike, accepted, politically correct, manly, cool, etc. to have and show emotions. If you were told as a baby, "Yes, please, cry all you want and as loudly as you want. And, while you're at it, save your biggest cries for the airplane ride home from Grandma's" you can skip this section. If not, do read on!

We need to understand that tears are nature's cleansing salts. Those who told us that it was not okay to have or express sadness were coming from their understanding of life based on what they were taught. Those caregivers learned to be uncomfortable with experiencing and expressing their own emotions by their caregivers and all of that has been projected downward through the lineage onto us. We have to accept—and for true growth, even love—both our ancestors and their past. We're not here to judge or change anyone else. But like all great generations, we can learn from the actions of those who came before us and forge onward with more awareness, all while feeling great compassion and gratitude. Their pain has led to our own emotional and spiritual progress. For that, I say, "Thank you."

Sadly; however, in addition to our early conditioning, parts of our consciously chosen spiritual path may also lead us to suppress our emotions. For instance, the Law of Attraction—a staple in New Thought / New Age worlds—tells us to focus solely on what we wish to experience. In effect, they say to focus on love and light or things we want rather than feel the pain of loss or anger or what we don't have. While there is some value to this overall, I believe it is a form of selective denial. Worse, it is misleading and ultimately unhealthy. If we're sad about something, whether it's our own grief or that of another that we're carrying, it is better to recognize and release that—*in addition* to focusing primarily on what we wish to have or experience. If we're spending one to two hours a week releasing, it's not going to open a floodgate and keep us stuck in the mire of depression; in fact, it's just the opposite. Like a good gardener, we have to both **plant new seeds and pull out the old weeds!** This relatively brief focus on getting in touch with and releasing the so-called negative within can free us. It keeps us compassionate and openhearted.

The Universe wants to give us the best of everything, including opportunities for spiritual growth and fulfillment. But if we're stuck in emotional and energetic denial, stagnation, stubbornness or resistance, little good seems to show up. And sometimes when something good does appear, our learned attachments to how we think it should look blocks our perception of it. We do not recognize it and instead wonder why the Universe is unfair. Then some of us resort to blaming others, or we await our big break to magically show up out of a sense of entitlement for having done so much spiritual work and being so wonderful. When we live mindfully we can clear the emotional issues as they arise. We become healthier and more whole, and blessings rain down upon us.

Healing Mindfully

Living mindfully includes a whole new approach to healing old, unresolved wounds, that perhaps can best be called healing mindfully. In the past, many of us believed that to clear an old wound, we need to re-live old painful experiences by recreating them in our mind's eye. While I have seen and have heard of this being effective, I wondered how necessary that is and more importantly, *why* it works, especially considering how many of us are told to believe that we must only focus on the positive. But we know from above that we must pull out the weeds AND plant new seeds, right? Well, that still eaves the *why*. Other methods of pulling weeds that I've seen and experienced are attempts to act out our deepest fears and pains. These include: yelling out one's anger, perhaps by expressing that energy toward someone who has volunteered to stand in for someone you have anger toward. Other methods are banging a plastic bat against a soft cushion or large malleable block while verbalizing fears and resentments. These forced emotional releases of grief about long lost lovers, family members or particular situations can be effective. Other scenarios can include acting out your darkest self, being arrogant or verbally abusive to a volunteer who understands their role in the recreated drama. There are numerous alternative therapies that posit that we must endure hours, years, or decades of talking it out, acting it out, and screaming and crying to release the repressed emotions. And there's nothing wrong with any of that. If it works for you, go for it! But please do so alongside a trained professional. AKA, do no try this at home.

So, while I do believe there is some benefit to expressing those pent up emotions, I posit that more is happening than we're commonly told. The linear thinking left brain in me doesn't like to just accept things as facts because someone else tells me it is so. Or worse, because a book allegedly written thousands of years ago or even last week tells me that something is true. So while I question what seems so, I also try to remain open-minded and expand the awareness to include other ways of living and being our true essence of love.

It is clear that as we progress, so does our understanding of what is it that heals and what is necessary to provide a space where healing can occur. Remember, what used to be considered factual is continually updated and usurped with more modern understandings. So *in addition to* and *not instead of* more traditional therapies and modalities when they're needed, I have found the most powerful healing force of the Universe to be acceptance and unconditional love— the energy of Source. In fact, I dare to say that unconditional love is the only thing that truly transforms anything on a deep causal level.

We should still take advantage of other systems where medically indicated; do not call me if you've broken your leg. Do not try to focus on acceptance and unconditional love when you're in an acute and potentially dangerous situation. Go to a hospital, get the bone set, take the antibiotic, etc., and thank your nurses and doctors, and **then** call me.

Acting out or re-experiencing fear or anger and other repressed energies that have manifested as wounds and pain and illness gives rise to the opposite, the acceptance and unconditional love of the Source. As we come to realize we all have a dark shadow self that is typically pushed down like a beach ball under the water, we create more room for healing. We spend lots of energy keeping this beach ball underwater and often do a pretty good job, but once in a while, the proverbial straw breaks the camel's back and we have an emotional outburst that we didn't even know we were capable of. A typically accepted and known example might be road rage. By witnessing this in ourselves in a controlled environment, we can better have compassion for others and ourselves. And that, to me, is the main difference between just acting out repressed emotions and truly healing them. It's not just *feel it to heal it*. It's *feel it, accept it, and love it to heal it!*

By knowing about and/or experiencing our darkness, we can better accept and unconditionally love others' perceived negative actions because we are more aware that there's no difference between them and us. Everyone has all sides— light and dark and everything in between—and the better we can accept our own full selves, the easier to accept others. Seeing the shadow is a humbling, if not frightful place that the mind will not want you to witness. The mind will resist almost all attempts to let this dark shadow self be seen, for it has been trained to keep darkness in the dark, and that it's expression would lead to both self criticism and others not liking us any longer. Well, we're already self critical and there are already many who don't like us, and we're still okay.

If you don't think you are capable of heinous feelings or acts, look up the Stanford Prison Experiment, where peace-loving hippies turned into physically and emotionally abusive monsters within a day, given a certain set of situations. If someone was attacking your loved one, you would likely do whatever it took to defend him or her, you may even kill an attacker if that's what it took. I can't imagine even he who is considered the holiest among us to just stand by idly and allow a loved one to experience an attack. This fierce, dark side has to be befriended in order for us to heal. I don't think we actually have to experience it as much as accept and love it. The emotional release techniques above-mentioned give rise to releasing of energy, but until those dark shadow selves are embraced and loved, they still own us. They can be expressed repeatedly and it can and often times does catalyze some changes, but just like a crying baby, what they really need is to be loved.

I have found that there is no better healer than unconditional love. This is the energy of the Universe, and all we have to do is connect to that and let that in through whatever means we can.

In my sessions, there often is conversation, and sharing of awareness and tools. This is to better understand the causal levels so that my clients have the knowledge and the tools to prevent new maladies from occurring as well as to ensure the older ones do not reoccur. In addition, typically, sessions also include time in silence. While this time can be called energy healing or mutual meditation, what's actually happening is that my client is experiencing unconditional love from the creator through me, a mindful type of healing. Because I am a relatively clear vessel, the love of Source pours through me and into my client. (I have met completely clear vessels only a couple of times and their presence filled me with so much pure love that it brought me to tears!) I am not the healer, but more a funnel of unconditional love. Source knows what we're working on and gives healing gifts in accordance with that intention. Clients have shared that they've experienced: bliss; partial to total emotional or physical pain relief; seen deceased relatives; met Jesus; had an out of body/Samadhi experience, and so much more. And all they had to do was to be open to this method of healing, and be willing to integrate what no longer serves them so that same energy no longer runs them. As much as my scientific side of my brain hates to say it, belief and willingness are the engine and catalyst of healing through this method. It is helpful, though not totally necessary to believe in a conscious, unconditionally loving Universe.

If a client maintains a Western paradigm of healthcare that only propagates physical body healing through medications or surgery, the short-term results may be wonderful, but the long-term results may not be, because they are adding trauma to more trauma. This is not an excuse to avoid surgery, but rather an invitation. When I had a small sebaceous cyst removed, the doctor couldn't believe how fast I healed, and it is my belief that an unusually quick recovery was able to happen because I filled my mind, heart, and body with gratitude and unconditional love both before during and after the surgery. If my client has no belief that Source is benevolent and actually wants to help us heal, or is resistant to that possibility, the results may be affected by that. And of course, if someone does not want to heal through this method or even Western healthcare, they won't. Yes, it's true; some are very attached to their pains and illness and wear them like a badge on a sleeve. Not you of course, I mean the other guy! Not even medications or surgeries have 100% effectiveness; there are too many variables. The variables could be: doctor (in)competence; (im)proper diagnosis; toxicity of or lack of adherence to prescription use; an attachment to being the wounded child, and more. The latter can manifest as illness after illness because the inner child's needs are only met superficially through well-intentioned medical practitioners and caregivers; the inner child is not given what truly heals at the core level!

In mindful healing, technically, most of what I'm doing is just being. I have no medical doctorate, no formal training in Western medicine, and only some in the Eastern healing arts, but as Tony Robbins said about himself that I'll borrow for a moment, I have a PhD in life. And so do many of you. You've seen your shadow self. You know it exists. Knowing this increases your compassion quotient and makes you a clearer vessel because you no longer judge those before you. And to me, that is the mark of a great healer. This higher vibration living allows you to be a super powerful conductor of Source energy if you let it. If you allow it, Source can work through you to transform many lives, including your own. It takes trust and surrender, and those are accomplished through practice, experience, and being in touch with a deeper knowing. As Oprah Winfrey said,

"Don't you think that God's plans for you are much bigger than your plans for you?" So why not get in touch with those plans and let them in?

I know this because my most dramatic healings and transformations happened when I released my own mind's ideas of who to be, and how to be. I listened when the signs became so clear that I no longer had a choice. And all of these relatively choiceless choices have turned out to be my best ones, and ironically, they weren't even my own.

Active Release of Grief
(I used to think I was bad for making people cry, now I get paid for it.)

So many of us are carrying grief. Keeping it in is dangerous; it must exit in some way to no longer hold its grip on you. An **active release** of grief would be crying it out with conscious intention. Some of us can do this on our own, but most need a guide. A trained or highly intuitive practitioner can create and hold sacred, safe space for us by phone or in person, allowing us to go deeper into—not away from—the grief. A lot of progress can be made in just an hour or two a week. On our own or in addition to sessions with a guide, we can start with 15 minutes a day sitting in silence and inviting what's already there and its accompanying message to make itself known. As we experience the emotion and embrace it and the message, it loses its charge, and the grief and grief-related symptoms begin to dissipate. And the more open we are to feeling the brief and temporary emotion or symptom and embracing it and its message, the more quickly and easily it will surface and dissipate. Willingness is key. Resistance is the block.

But be careful not to force it. Better to open and allow it. Forcing is the mind's idea, allowing is the soul's. Meet it head on with unconditional love and acceptance. It's beautifully human, and like any living thing, requires love.

If you are concerned about "opening the floodgates" once you face your buried emotions, consider the following: A 51-year-old woman spent a good portion of three consecutive months crying. She was so overcome with feeling her grief that she couldn't work during that time. It would be logical to assume she'd lose a lot during that time, and she did. She lost about 20 pounds; she lost the wrinkles on her face, and she lost the gray in her hair. She finalized a split with her partner and gave up her home. Looking and feeling about 15 years younger, she then took a vacation. While overseas, she met someone who offered her a well-paying job doing what she loves to do, on the continent on which she was born—where she had wanted to return but couldn't afford to. This is one of the most extreme cases I have ever seen of an extended and consistent emotional release, and it led to an equally powerful, positive outcome. But none if it was forced; it was all allowed and even embraced. And because she had a supportive network of friends and practitioners who understood this, she felt safe enough to 'go there.'

Passive Release of Grief

The other option for releasing repressed emotions and energy, which most tend to prefer, is a **passive release**. Most energy healing is effective, given the following elements in the client's awareness: conscious intention; belief in the modality; a willingness to heal; surrender; and openness to the support of the loving Universe.

Passive healing begins with an awareness that our bodies and the Universe are always giving us what we need and that all we really need to do is allow it to happen. Think about a common kitchen cut you may receive from sloppily slicing vegetables. At most, you'll apply an adhesive bandage; you KNOW it will heal in a few days regardless of what you do. What would happen if we knew on an equal level that our bodies are always trying to self-heal even "major" pains and illness?

Inner Column Healing

While doing this, connect to what I call the Inner Column of Light. I envision a tube of light, along the spinal cord, as my Inner Source. It goes up and out of the head to the heavens as well as downward to the Earth. Instead of pushing or pulling at the resistance or the repressed energy, as is done in many of the aforementioned modalities, I find it more powerful to connect with that Inner Column, and invite what ails you to fall off naturally. Pushing or pulling or forcing is another form of resistance, and I just have not found that to be in our best interests. It may seem like it will take longer using this method, but I'd rather take a longer period of time and be more effective over the long haul than have short repeated bursts of clarity followed by even more confusion and frustration.

Although most of us think we would prefer a passive release of emotional energy because it sounds "easier" than active release, we need to remember that it takes trust and surrender for that to happen. Surrender means to give up your own ideas of what healing should look like, and embrace what shows up in the moment.

Working with a Practitioner

If the Creator wanted us to experience life on our own, he/she/it would have created seven billion planets; one person each. Sessions with a practitioner are highly advised for maximum efficiency. They can involve both active and passive releases. As we get better at what we're doing and as trust is formed, the release becomes easier because the emotional walls of protection come down. This is where a practitioner who listens from the heart often comes into play. If we are heard from the heart, the seat of compassion, we feel safer than if we fear we are being heard from a mind that is inclined to judge and make personal recommendations and judgments. There's nothing wrong with words of wisdom, but similar to the above-described recalibration, the healing happens in the silence.

Anger

Releasing anger is also done actively or passively. What, you don't do anger? Spiritual people don't have anger? This is what most of us are taught. Even without spiritual training, modern culture conditions us not to express our anger. How many of you were told when you were younger, "Yes, please, express your anger in whatever way feels right to you, and even better, save your tantrums for when we're in a restaurant?"

Again: I thought so.

We need to get real. Anger is not a bad thing; but the repression of anger is a horrible thing—unless we like road rage, elevated blood pressure, and tumors. Yes, everyone gets angry. We all have anger and it needs to come out for ultimate health and spiritual connection. Until we reach God-consciousness, or enlightenment, we will experience anger. But if we selectively bury that emotion, severe energy blockages form and create unhealthy and unpleasant symptoms. We have to acknowledge that we hold anger in our bodies and then allow it to surface and heal.

If you're "too spiritual" to have or express anger, you've been force-fed a version of spirituality that will keep you coming back for more healing that doesn't really heal, despite it's potential claims of setting you free. In any moment, given certain circumstances, any of us can behave like Hitler or the Dalai Lama. Full awareness and acceptance of both our light and our dark sides is paramount for total expression and health.

Releasing Anger

Remember, we can heal with intention and right action. Wrong action would be to yell at someone who's angered us. That is one ego trying to change or outdo another ego. The other ego will likely be ignited and no one wins in a battle of egos. When we embrace and release the emotional charge, we can have a civil conversation with another person, connect more deeply with them, share our true experience, and know we are being heard. But if the damaged ego—AKA the pain body—is leading the conversation, we should expect nothing good to come of it.

An effective **active** release of anger is doing physical activity with a clear intention to release anger—not aiming the anger at its supposed human cause. I play tennis sometimes with that intention and when I hit the ball into the next county, my coach knows I'm in a self-therapy session and allows it to happen. Some people "bash." They write down a characteristic or an experience that caused them anger on an index card, and beat it mercilessly with a plastic bat until the card is in shreds. We can also hit a couch with a tennis racket, etc. All of these are best done with a practitioner or coach at our side to assure our safety and that of anyone around us. He or she will also push us when we feel like giving up or when self-judgments scream inside our head,

"Spiritual people don't do anger" or "I'm bad if I get angry." Like "hitting the wall" while running but pushing through to catch our second wind, a release of anger often can be just one more step away. But because it can be a really difficult and uncomfortable step, we tend to think we're done before we really are. A good guide will know when enough really is enough or if we need an extra push. Again, remember to release it, embrace it, and love it to transform it. Love not only the anger but the process of its creation and the journey it took to get you to release it. Don't worry about where it goes, the Universe will soak it up and transform it, especially when it's released with love and not self-criticism for having gotten angry in the first place.

Anger also can be released **passively**. Lying in a safe energetic bubble created by a skilled guide, surrounded by the love of Source with healing intention, we can sense our anger lifting up and out. We once again connect to the Inner Column of Light, our Inner Source, and again, with more surrender, acceptance and love, there is more healing. The more we're ready, willing, and able to let go of old grudges—our own and ones we have taken on from others—the easier and quicker the healing. This is forgiveness, manifested. This is healing.

Conclusion

The human mind will opt out of anything uncomfortable. It has been doing so since we were children. But we're not children any longer. It's time to take responsibility for replacing old patterns with newer ones. It's time to step into our greatness and our birthright of unconditional love and optimal health. The journey can at times be uncomfortable, but it's necessary. The more we open and embrace any resistance, the less uncomfortable it will be.

We cannot deny the existence of lower-vibration energies stuck within us any longer. We each have 60 to 100 trillion cells within us and, even as cells are replaced constantly with new ones, the memories of this lifetime live on. And our spiritual DNA may carry memories of prior lifetimes! Some therapies posit that we need to fully revisit unpleasant memories to clear them. I agree that repressed emotion or energy must be brought to the surface for expression and healing, but the process doesn't always have to be a messy, rage- or tear-filled affair. While that route can be helpful, it is not mandatory. To heal, we needn't know about every injury, betrayal, abandonment, relationship gone wrong, etc., throughout our soul's existence. We can heal now with surrender and by following the "Steps to Healing Empathic Pain and Illness."

1. Know you're not responsible for the soul of anyone else; and be mindful of your true intentions underneath any actions;

2. Let harmful energies pass through you as opposed to keeping them using the Keyhole;

3. Become aware of what's being stored; if it's yours, another's or a combination, using the Body Scan;

4. Release negative energy that has already accumulated with the Return to Sender exercise for as many people and situations are necessary; and

5. Recalibrate to the higher vibration

If you have difficulties with this material, or wish to share about your experience with it, please contact me. From my heart to yours, thank you for reading, for sharing, and for being you.

About Dave's Services

Many of us are already aware that repressed emotions cause energy blockages that create pain and illness, and that illness will not heal without working with the causative energy. I've been helping move the repressed energy in others for years, and have an extremely high success rate in co-facilitating permanent transformations by identifying and working with the underlying causes. If you're not well-informed or experienced in this concept, please read my book, *Healing with Source: A Spiritual Guide to Mind-Body Medicine,* published by Findhorn Press. (You can read the first 30 pages for free at my website.) *Healing with Source* has 174 pages of eye-opening information and action steps to becoming your own medical intuitive and reversing pain and illness by intuiting and releasing the underlying, emotional, and energetic cause(s). Some of you may have already read that and were ready for more info, so thanks for reading this one, too.

The work that I do can be done via phone or in person and works wonderfully to passively release energy and repressed emotions, and also provides a safe space for a more active release. I also can intuit words of wisdom to help you gain clarity about most situations, even those beyond typical emotional or physical pain and illness.

Please stay in touch with me for more books, video, and workshops, and to schedule private sessions. Sign up for my monthly newsletter so we can stay in touch and can share the latest healing techniques, success stories, and more at website, www.DaveMarkowitz.Com. If this material inspires you, please tell a friend or two, or twenty.

13149805R00067

Made in the USA
San Bernardino, CA
11 July 2014